FROM THE FLIGHT DECK

April 2017

Avery

Keep Super Good!

Cmdr Petters

FROM THE
FLIGHT DECK

~

Thoughts on Sales, Life, and Personal Development

ALEX PETTES

iUniverse, Inc.
Bloomington

From the Flight Deck
Thoughts on Sales, Life, and Personal Development

iUniverse books may be ordered through booksellers or by contacting:

iUniverse
1663 Liberty Drive
Bloomington, IN 47403
www.iuniverse.com
1-800-Authors (1-800-288-4677)

ISBN: 978-1-4502-8158-4 (sc)
ISBN: 978-1-4502-8076-1 (ebk)

Printed in the United States of America

iUniverse rev. date: 01/06/2011

To my girls, Tabitha and Nicole. I always told you that you would have the weirdest dad of all your friends. Daddy loves you.

To my wife, Tammy. I love you more now than I did when we got married. Thank you for your support in all I have done. I am who I am because of you.

Contents

Preface

I have wanted to write a book for quite some time now. I actually started with a blank journal on January 2, 2005, and planned on this being my idea journal. I recorded some ideas, and the next entry, on December 31, 2005, started with "Here I am again, one year later reflecting on the past year and wondering why I made no progress on this book?" I guess I was not ready then, but now I think I am. What is different?

In February 2009, I made a decision that I would actually commit to writing a book. I had publically declared this to many people, so I could not go back on my word! And for a variety of reasons, I think I was ready to actually begin the process. On April 2, 2009, I started an "Idea Canvas" (more on this later), where I visually recorded ideas and insights as I discovered them, and that was the real catalyst for what you now hold.

The book is primarily written for me and my family, as part of my personal journey of discovery. I hope that whoever reads it can glean a few nuggets of wisdom from the pages within. I have been a student of the science of personal development for almost twenty years, starting when I was offered to become the General Sales Manager of Atlantic Speedy Propane in October of 1991. I had never been in sales before, and that new position started my journey on the road to self-discovery and wisdom. I am thankful that my first foray in the world of personal development led me to Zig Ziglar, as much of what I have learned from Zig comprises who I am today.

From Zig I first realized that there is no such thing as a self-made person. All of us have had help along the way. And if you believe as Malcolm Gladwell wrote in his book *Outliers*, our personal and cultural history has a big impact on where we are today. I hope that what follows does justice to those whom I have learned from and imparts some of what I have discovered along the way to those who will read this.

If nothing else, the journey of this book writing has been of benefit to me, and for that I am thankful. I have been blessed my entire life, and I hope this book blesses you as well.

Introduction: Who Is Commander Pettes?

I have been known as Commander (Cmdr) Pettes since 2000. But who is Cmdr Pettes? Cmdr Pettes is the persona that I have used for over ten years when I have done sales meetings or training for the company I am now President and co-owner of, TFI Food Equipment Solutions (TFI). TFI is a specialty restaurant equipment distributor located in Brampton, Ontario, Canada, a city near Toronto. The Cmdr Pettes persona is a *Top Gun*–style military fighter pilot. Whenever I do a Cmdr Pettes presentation, I come out with the music of *Top Gun* blaring, dressed in my uniform of a military flight suit, parachute harness, and my fully painted fighter pilot helmet. Cmdr Pettes is the Sales Fighter Pilot Squadron Leader of the USS TFI. And Cmdr Pettes has also become my personal "brand."

I have consciously developed this brand and identity through a number of marketing efforts and materials. I have had my youngest daughter develop a series (now three) of personalized thank-you cards that she designed, all with Cmdr Pettes imagery of various sorts. If I meet you for the first time

Alex Pettes

and get your address, you will get one of these cards. The envelope is even mailed with a Cmdr Pettes postage stamp! My license plate reads "THE CMDR," and in my home is a 6' X 8' painting that my wife, Tammy, and I commissioned of a country scene, with a house on a hill, surrounded by vineyards and a gentle stream rolling down the front. The words "Pettes Winery" are labelled on a stack of wine barrels in front of the house. And in the top right hand corner, coming out of the clouds, is the Cmdr Pettes fighter jet!

A selection of Cmdr Pettes thank-you cards and stamps.

So where did all this start? In grade eleven, I had been involved in Junior Achievement (JA) for two years already. JA allows high school students to start up and run a business for a twenty-six-week period, starting with raising capital by selling shares, developing and creating a product, manufacturing and

4

selling it, and eventually producing a shareholders' report and winding up the company. In my third year at JA, I was elected President of GEMCO, one of about twenty JA companies in our area. Our company was sponsored and advised by employees of the local GM plant in St. Catharines, Ontario. Part of being President meant presiding over our quarterly (every six weeks) board meeting for the whole company (about twenty or so Achievers). In my third board meeting, I came up with the idea of using a skit to present our board meeting message. It was based on *Star Trek*, and I was Captain Pettes.

"Free Enterprise, the final frontier. These are the voyages of the Starship *GEMCO*. Its eight-month mission: to learn about and experience Canada's free enterprise system, to have fun and to make a profit for ourselves and our shareholders. President's Log, Stardate Liquidation Week. We are now on the last leg of our journey after a successful mission in the St. Catharines Solar System …"

One of our advisors (the adult supervisors), Walt Hambrock, joined me in the skit. He was Admiral Walt and sent us a message from Starfleet Command. He popped up in the window in the wall as if he were on a view screen and gave us a message for our final week's journey. This is the first time I can remember ever using an alter ego to get my message across. And I have kept it up ever since.

I don't know why I kept coming back to these various personas to get my message across. Actually, that is not true. I do know. Number one, I loved doing them! Number two, they proved to be extremely effective in conveying the message. I really started using them in earnest when I was working as a product manager for Garland Commercial Ranges, a commercial cooking equipment manufacturer. I was responsible for a number of brands of equipment that Garland distributed in Canada for its sister companies.

At one of the first sales meetings as product manager, I was introducing a new ice machine brand called Ice-O-Matic. I came into the room dressed in a gas mask, wearing a combat helmet with Ice-O-Matic stickers on it and shooting foam projectiles from my Nerf gun. The message was that we need to "take the beach" and sell the compact Ice-O-Matic under-counter ice machine and get it on our dealers' sales floors. If were able to establish a beachhead with this product, we would be able to get our dealers to buy the bigger machines. I still have the photos of all the sales guys wearing the helmet that sales meeting! They really got a kick out of the presentation.

The next sales meeting we had, following up on the "take the beach" theme, I gave out a small award for those who had achieved their targets. And even more fun, I handed out kids' plastic pails and shovels to those who did not achieve their targets and thought that "take the beach" meant play in the sand! They got the message and everyone had a laugh at seeing them pose with their toys!

The following year, I was introducing another new line to the sales staff, Lincoln Impinger pizza ovens and Wear Ever pots and pans. This time I came in dressed like Dan Aykroyd from the Blues Brothers and came as Brother Pettes. I think I had discovered that people like someone who is willing to have fun, and these personas started became part of who I was, or as I discovered later, they became my brand.

A year or so later, in about 1998, I first started using the fighter pilot persona that I have carried on with to this day. Captain Pettes, the marketing fighter pilot from the USS Garland was born! It all started in my new role as the product manager for the Range and Specialty Products Division of Garland. We made commercial ranges (stoves), grills, broilers, and other heavy-duty cooking equipment. We were transforming our manufacturing division into a new, more modern operation. It was from that idea that I developed the fighter pilot analogy. I came up with the idea that Garland was in the midst of transforming itself from a 1940s-era battleship into a twenty-first-century aircraft carrier! Battleships won the last wars, but today, modern aircraft carriers are the key to victory, and so the analogy was that we needed to transform ourselves to keep up our leadership position in our industry. I was Captain Pettes, the fighter pilot who got to fly off the ship (leave the factory) and travel around the world visiting customers and distributors to help market our products. So I developed this persona, down to the flight suit (a pair of blue coveralls), a real pilot helmet, and a parachute harness that I bought at the army surplus and started coming into meetings to the music of *Top Gun*!

A drawing of Captain Pettes of the USS *Garland*, which one of the factory employees drew for me.

At first, I did the Captain Pettes presentations for the plant factory employees at our quarterly meetings. They loved it, as they had never had any presentation made to them like this before! I would come in and tell them what was happening in the world with our products and what our customers were saying about what they were producing. After I began to do these presentations, as I would walk the aisles of the plant, many guys would stop and salute Captain Pettes as I walked by! I not only started to introduce Captain Pettes to our own sales force but always without fail did a Captain Pettes presentation with the various dealer sales force trainings we had at the plant. That started my more public persona and brand as Captain Pettes outside the Garland employees.

Over time (and I must admit, due to the overwhelming positive reinforcement and feedback I got every time I did a Captain Pettes presentation), I got better and more comfortable in this role. I started to expand the scope of what Captain Pettes represented. In October of 2000, I won one of five President's Awards given out at our annual management meeting for Garland. This was a peer-voted award, and as such meant a great deal to me. The next morning at the opening session of the day's events, the VP of Sales, Jeff Couch, said, "Well, since Alex won the President's Award last night, I think he deserves a promotion from Captain Pettes to Commander Pettes." And Cmdr Pettes it has been ever since!

In December 2000, I left Garland and joined TFI Food Equipment Solutions, a specialty restaurant equipment distributor, as the VP of sales and marketing. In June 2006, I became President of TFI. Many of my peers wanted to know what my new rank would be, now that I was President.

"So Alex, are you now Admiral Pettes?"

I responded, "No, I am still The Cmdr, but my title is now Cmdr-in-Chief!" And I have the business cards to prove it!

Over the years, as I have evolved, so has my Cmdr Pettes persona. Now when I do a Cmdr Pettes presentation, it is usually to a sales or sales management audience. Every TFI sales meeting I have had since I started in December 2000 has started with Cmdr Pettes making his entrance. I talk about why salespeople are like fighter pilots, as the two are remarkably similar.

Why Are Salespeople Like Fighter Pilots?

What makes an effective sales fighter pilot? I have developed this as a pyramid of four levels, each building on the one below it. It starts with the foundation of being "calm, confident, and yet slightly cocky." Not arrogance, but the calm, controlled confidence of a well-trained and competent professional.

The second level is "knows the equipment, environment, competition and the mission." This speaks to the requirement of having knowledge, goals, and the plan for your actions. Fighter pilots (and effective people) don't just fly around hoping to bump into opportunity. They have a plan for achievement.

The third level is based on being "ever learning, ever improving." Brian Tracy said, "You will be the same tomorrow as you are today except for the books your read and the people you meet." Education does not stop when you finish school. "Green and growing or ripe and rotting" was a favourite expression of Ray Kroc, founder of McDonald's. Always be ready to learn and develop.

Finally, it is topped off with the "whatever it takes" winning attitude. An appropriate pyramid for a sales person, but also for anyone who wants to lead a meaningful life.

I have been fortunate to have presented to audiences literally around the world as Cmdr Pettes. I have spoken to customers throughout the United States, Canada, England, Australia, and New Zealand when I was with Garland. Since joining TFI, I have spoke at many of our distributor meetings to international audiences in Italy, South Africa, and throughout the United States. And for the past five years or so, I have done the full Cmdr Pettes presentation to Professor Herb MacKenzie's fourth-year sales management class at Brock University, where I graduated in 1987. That one, I think, turns me on more than all the rest, as these students have no clue about what they are in for; they are at the start of their professional careers and I hope that what I say makes an impact. In any event, "the teacher learns more than the student," and I get so much out of getting ready for the presentation that the preparation alone makes it worthwhile for me.

So who is Cmdr Pettes? Over time, I have developed my own personal mission statement that I repeat aloud every day (yep, every day) three times. It is the essence of who I am, what I aspire to be, and my vision for the future. My mission statement:

Cmdr Pettes' Mission Statement

"I AM the Commander. I AM the Leader at the Front. I AM the most positive, enthusiastic, vibrant person, who loves God and his family and continually contributes in the service to others.
I AM having everything in life I want as I help and serve enough other people get what they want."

As I have thought about and repeated this mission statement for over five years now, I am ever more convinced that this really is my personal goal and the ideal for which I am striving. What is the reason for a mission statement? It is a driving force, an overriding objective, a fixed point that all your actions and activities can be guided toward and judged by. My mission is to be a leader. To love God and my family (in that priority order) and most importantly, to serve others. This mission statement is positive, using the assertive statement "I AM." It is motivating, as it gives me the reasons for why I am doing what I am doing. And it is rooted in the oldest laws of the universe: The law of sowing and reaping. The law of cause and effect. The golden rule.

The last sentence exhorts that I AM having everything I want if I just help enough others first. Serve first, contribute to others and by the wondrous laws of nature I will get everything I want. It is not a material pledge (although material gain can be expected.) Victor Hugo said, "Life is to give, not to take."

I want to give and serve of myself to others. Mohammad said, "He is best among humans who is best at repaying." I want to repay for all the blessings I have received, and in doing so, the mysterious benefit is that life reciprocates back to me many times more.

Earl Nightingale's wisdom from his classic, *The Strangest Secret* says, "You become what you think about." This wisdom, popularized in the twentieth century, is actually over five thousand years old. The ancient sages of India wrote a number of Upanishads, or "instructions at the feet of the master." The Maitri Upanishad says, "The transmigration of life takes place in one's own mind. Let one therefore keep the mind pure, for what a man thinks, that he becomes. This is a mystery of Eternity."

As I think about my personal mission and repeat it every day, I hope I am becoming one who wants to serve others first. I hope so. That I think is why I was led to write this book. I hope it is not perceived as just a self-serving recording of what Alex has done, as truly I have a positive self-image and do not need external reinforcement. I hope it offers the reader a number of nuggets of wisdom that are picked up and used and thus helps them become just a little bit better off having read this book. "Take the best, forget the rest." You won't hurt my feelings.

Notes from the Idea Canvas

Once I had conceived the idea for this book, I wanted to find a way to record the various ideas and insights that might be useful when I finally got around to the actual writing. I had a journal that I was using, but I am a visual person and needed something "in my face" to keep me motivated.

I was reading a blog by a great marketing writer named Seth Godin. He referenced an artist named Hugh MacLeod's blog, so I clicked on the link and kept reading. One of things on the blog was a regular update on Hugh's progress as he created a piece of art. This art was a canvas that was becoming ever more filled with what I think was small detailed words in black ink.

Suddenly, the idea came to me.

So on April 2, 2009, I went out to the art store and bought a 28" X 32" blank framed canvas and hung it on the wall in my office at home. I bought four different-coloured Sharpie markers and that day started what I called my Idea Canvas. The concept was that anyone could add a thought or a note to the canvas. With the various colours of markers and the "random" method in which the various sayings would be written, not only would this be a great vehicle to keep ideas, but it would also end up as a piece of personal art.

My Idea Canvas, where I wrote thoughts, ideas, and inspiring quotes.

Over the next fourteen or so months, if I was reading and found a particularly interesting or inspiring thought, I recorded it on the canvas. I really got to like this simple idea. The Idea Canvas became significant to me in a few ways. First, it was a simple and inexpensive way to publically make sure I kept my word and wrote my book. Second, I often would review the items written down, further reinforcing the personal development journey and the lessons I was learning. Third, it became a conversation piece, and now that it is filled (although there is always space for more ideas!), I think it is quite an interesting piece of personal art and a part of me. I created the art for myself, but as with all art, the viewer can take away whatever message and meaning it creates for them. Whatever your feelings about it, you won't hurt mine!

Below I have recorded all the items written on the Idea Canvas. I have tried to order the random nature of these thoughts into a few helpful categories. As you read the variety and quantity of ideas below, I hope that you will find some that resonate with you. They are varied in nature and have been taken from many areas (I have tried to note the source where possible), along with comments from my kids and my nephews, who also added a few points. With each subsection, I will try to relay a summary of what the points mean to me. In this and all the following sections, the text written in point form is as it appears on the canvas. And the order in which the points appear has no real meaning or substance. They are random, like the ideas that came to me over time as I filled the canvas. Enjoy!

Ideas for the Book

As I started the Idea Canvas, the initial idea was to record some ideas that I might end up putting in the book. Below are the random ideas that came to me, some of which have actually ended up as chapters or as ideas that were developed further.

- Dog tags as chapter headings
- What is the objective of writing the book? Why? For Whom?

- The inspiration for this came from Hugh MacLeod's blog and his "DesertManhattan" art
- Remove the ego behind why and a better book and message will occur
- Cmdr Mission Statement
- I am thinking of *From the Flight Deck* as the book title
- Narrative hook
- Challenge Coins or CD/DVD
- A journey of personalities and influences I have encountered
- The Sailor, The Seal, and The Swami
- Lessons from the Mouse
- Chart of The Mastery Grid
- Lesson's from Mario

Comments from the Kids

Before I get too deep into the list of ideas, I wanted to start with the thoughts and ideas that were given by the kids. I wanted to have this Idea Canvas to be a way to involve others in the process of developing the book. While most of what the kids wrote is funny and light, there is definitely some wisdom in the words of these youth.

a. Tabitha Pettes (my oldest daughter)
- I have read *Holes* for every report I had in grade school. Make your book that good! I love you
- "Out damned spot, out!" Lady Macbeth
- Marry rich and you will live a good life
- Chapter Title: Tabitha, my Favourite Daughter

- Behind this canvas is everything you'll never understand
- Will it be first person or third person? That is the question
b. Nicole Pettes (my youngest daughter)
- The three little pigs is one of the most rewarded stories of all time!
- (A drawing of a heart with "I love you") Your book should symbolize something you are passionate about
- I see said the blind man to his deaf wife as his paralyzed children came running—Tell the truth in your book
- Men are like trees; it takes them 50 years to grow up
- A good friend will bail you out of jail. A true friend will be sitting next to you saying, "That was Awesome!"
- A hug is like a boomerang; you get it back right away
- Life without love is like a chocolate chip cookie without chocolate chips … boring
- "When you are in love, you have to share the 'starism'"
- "MMM. Sprinkles. Crunchy little balls of sugar"
- Goal setting triggers your subconscious computer
- Good things come from hard work
- Life is full of setbacks. Success is determined by how you react to them
c. Nephews
- Keep your ears open wider than your mouth (Tyler Marshall)
- If you see something, it doesn't mean it's not alive (Lucas Lafleur)

-   The road ends 2 ways; which one will you choose
    (Lucas Lafleur)

Service to Others

One of the themes that came out very clearly in the reading and thinking I did over the past couple of years was the nature of service to others. The idea that man's highest ideal is in service to others dates back thousands of years. It is interesting how the same message has pervaded the generations and has been stated in so many ways. I hope that many of these comments resonate and inspire you in some way.

-   "They also serve who only stand and wait." John
    Milton, "On His Blindness"
-   "Life is to give, not to take." Victor Hugo
-   "He is best among humans who is best at repaying."
    Mohammad
-   "Through service to the whole, we open our lives to
    a larger purpose." Judith Anodea, *Waking the Global
    Heart*
-   "This is mans highest end; to other's service all his
    powers to lend." Oedipus in Sophocles' *The Oedipus
    Trilogy*
-   "Make it your guiding principal to do your best
    for others and to be trust worthy in what you say."
    Confucius Book 1–8
-   "The era in which we live belongs to people who
    believe in themselves, but are focused on the needs
    of others." Jeff Immelt, CEO of GE

- "So in everything you do, do unto others what you would have them do unto you, for this sums up the Law and the Prophets." Jesus, Mathew 7:12
- "'Selje.' Norwegian for sell, which means 'to serve.' To sell means to serve." Zig Ziglar
- "The law of success is service; that we get what we give. And for this reason we should consider it a great privilege to be able to give." Charles Haanel, *The Master Key System*
- Be a hummingbird; do all you can!
- "Nobody makes a greater mistake than he who did nothing because he could only do a little." Edmund Burke

Self and Personal Development

I have considered myself a student of the science of personal development for many years. I owe much of my personal and professional success to the fact that at a young age of about twenty-six, I discovered a number of great teachers through books, most notably Zig Ziglar. Much of who I am I learned directly from the authors I read and listened to. And I did my best to try to put what I learned into action, as that is where true growth occurs and results show up.

- Discipline: "I have never accidentally eaten anything." Zig Ziglar
- "Nothing tastes as good as thin feels." Zig Ziglar
- Pursuit of an ideal or goal develops initiative, energy and enthusiasm

- Fighter pilot pyramid:

Whatever it takes!
Ever learning, improving
Know the mission, environment
Calm, confident, and yet slightly cocky

- "The quality of our life's journey can never be higher than the level of personal development we have attained." James Hollis, *Finding Meaning in the Second Half of Life*
- "If I had to pick a single indicator of a future top leader, I would say it's the degree of his commitment and determination to improve himself, on his own." General Tony Zinni, *Leading the Charge*
- "You can't build a garden with withered flowers; you must start within!" Mathieu Ricard
- "The greatest treasure humans can have is self confidence." Buddha
- "Whether you prevail or fail, endure or die, depends more on what you do to yourself than on what the world does to you." Jim Collins, *How the Mighty Fall and Why Some Companies Never Give In*
- "Therefore, everyone who hears these words of mine AND puts them into practice is like a wise man who builds his house on the rock." Jesus, Mathew 7:24
- "Persistence is self-discipline in action." Brian Tracy
- "I am responsible!" Greg McMaster, President, Taylor Company
- Pain is weakness leaving the body
- Take the Best, forget the Rest

- "I count him braver who overcomes his desires than him who conquers his enemies; for the hardest victory is over self." Aristotle

As You Think...

In the 1960s, a great simple book was written by Earl Nightingale called "The Strangest Secret." The premise he went on to talk about was that as humans, "we become what we think about." I listened to this book on tape over fifteen years ago, and it was a very powerful thought. Early in the twenty-first century, a compilation book by Rhonda Byrne called *The Secret* took the stage as a simple and powerful book for the modern age. Its premise is that The Secret is the Law of Attraction: what you think about, you will become. My first thought after reading this was to think that I had heard this already from Earl Nightingale. What a surprise to discover that this same message had been spoken by many sages thousands of years ago. Wisdom of the ages is truly ageless.

- "Be careful what you think, because your thoughts run your life." Proverbs 4:23
- "Let one therefore keep the mind pure, for what a man thinks, that he be becomes. This is a mystery of eternity." Maitri Upanishad, Indian sages from 5000 BC
- "All we are is a result of what we have thought." Buddha
- "All that a man achieves and all that he fails to achieve is the direct result of his own thoughts. As he thinks, so he is; as he continues to think, so he remains." James Allen, *As a Man Thinketh*

- "You become what you think about." Earl Nightingale, *The Strangest Secret*
- "Finally brothers, whatever is true, whatever is noble, whatever is right, whatever is pure, whatever is lovely, whatever is admirable—if anything is excellent or praiseworthy, think about such things." My baptism verse, June 2, 2002, Philippians 4:8
- "No experience is terrible unless you make it so." Plutarch
- "The Secret is The Law of Attraction: Ask-Believe-Receive." Rhonda Byrne *The Secret*
- Bad VERBs that weaken your Personal Power: Victimization; Entitlement; Rescue; Blame - All are focused on giving responsibility for your feelings and happiness to others. I AM Responsible!

Life Lessons

Many of the ideas and thoughts on the canvas could be considered Life Lessons. The quotes in this section did not really fit under the other headings, so I created a smaller chunk of wisdom to digest!

- Desire<Wealth = Riches: Desire>Wealth = Poverty
- To earn more, learn more
- Leisure is a luxury best enjoyed in small portions
- A life worth living is a life worth recording
- Weddings optional, funerals mandatory
- Life is full of setbacks: Success is determined by how you react to them

- Focus + Daily Improvement + Time = Genius - Robin Sharma 'The Greatness Guide'
- Trial + Error + Reflection+ Perseverance = Desired Result
- Gift + Passion = Better World

Little Lists for Life

I am a list person. I studied in school with lists, and I enjoy the simplicity of lists and the messages they convey. I had a number of lists that appeared on the canvas, some philosophical, some practical, and all worth reviewing.

- Think of 3 things:
    - Whence you came
    - Where you are going
    - To whom you must give account
        - Benjamin Franklin
- 3 requirements for meaningful work:
    - Relationship between effort and reward
    - Complexity
    - Autonomy
        - Malcolm Gladwell, *The Outliers*
- Body – Mind – Intellect – Self
- "Nine things you must do to succeed in love and life"
    - 1. Dig it up
    - 2. Pull your tooth
    - 3. Play the movie
    - 4. Do something
    - 5. Act like an ant

- o   6. Hate well
- o   7. Don't play fair
- o   8. Be humble
- o   9. Upset the right people
  - ▪   By Dr. Henry Cloud, *9 Things a Leader Must Do*
- Understanding the lessons of the pump will reveal the secrets of success!
  - o   1. Prime the pump – put in first
  - o   2. The deeper the water the purer it is – hard work is the sweetest
  - o   3. Don't stop! – the water goes down and you start over again
  - o   4. Once the water is flowing, a little easy, steady, pressure is all you need for the water to continue to flow
- The 3 basic interests in life:
  - o   Sense of purpose
  - o   Health
  - o   Relationships (others and God)
- The 3 C's to success:
  - o   Concentration
  - o   Consistency
  - o   Co-operation
    - ▪   Swamiji Parthasarathy
- The masculine journey:
  - o   Boyhood
  - o   Cowboy
  - o   Warrior
  - o   Lover
  - o   King

- o   Sage
  - ▪   John Eldridge, *Fathered by God*
- 3 Universal reasons for working:
  - o   Survive
  - o   Save
  - o   Serve
    - ▪   Bob Burg and John David Mann, *The Go-Giver*

Wisdom Proverbs and Great Quotes

There are many great quotes, and the vast majority of the ideas I ended up writing down on the canvas were quotes. I could not sort these into nicer, smaller chunks of thought. Review this list more slowly, as each quote bears the seed of a great tree of wisdom.

- "Forgiveness is the fragrance the violet releases as the foot crushes it." Mark Twain
- "Men will not die for gold, but men will die for ribbons." Napoleon
- "Where wealth accumulates, men decay." Oliver Goldsworth
- "But they whom truth and wisdom lead, can gather honey from a weed." William Cowper, "The Pineapple and the Bee"
- "The greatest burden a child must bear is the unlived lives of their parents." Carl Jung.
- "I promise to live a great, full life and relieve my girls of this burden." Alex Pettes
- "Blessed are all who fear the Lord, who walk in His ways. You will eat the fruit of your labour. Blessings and prosperity will be yours!" Psalm 128: 1–2

- "Symbol and metaphor are our greatest gifts, for they make culture and spirituality possible." James Hollis, *Finding Meaning in the Second Half of Life*
- "All that matters in the end is how we love." Beth Neilson Chapman
- "To her lover, a beautiful woman is a delight. To an ascetic, a distraction. To a wolf, a good meal." Zen poem
- "He who loves does not dispute." Lao Tzu
- "It is more worthwhile to take care of our mind than to only take care of our money." Dalai Lama, *The Compassionate Life*
- "Walk on one foot of risk, then on one foot of mastery. You must walk on both." Dawna Markova
- "If anyone wants to be first, he must be the very last and the servant of all." Jesus, Mark 9:35
- "He who receives an idea from me, receives instruction himself without lessening mine, as he who lights his taper (candle) at mine, receives light without darkening me." Thomas Jefferson
- "Great is truth. Fire cannot burn nor water drown it."
- "He who has a partner has a master." Italian Proverb.
- "All human wisdom is summed in two words; wait and hope." Alexandre Dumas, *The Count of Monte Cristo*
- "Knowledge is not given; it is taken." Swamiji Parthasarathy
- "Eternal vigilance is the price of success." Charles Haanel, *The Master Key System*
- "Opinion without knowledge is always a poor thing." Plato, *The Symposium*

- "A little bit of fragrance always clings to the hand that gives you roses." Chinese proverb
- "Though the sun is not itself sight, it is the cause of sight and is seen by the sight it causes." Plato, The Allegory of the Cave
- "Too much or too little light blinds you (to truth)." Antoni Gaudi on design of the windows in the La Sagrada Familia church in Barcelona
- "If you want to be happier, do more of the things that make you happy." Robin Sharma, *The Greatness Guide*
- "I never met a rich pessimist." Ned Goodman
- "Follow the thread to what is next, but hold the thread with a subtle hand." Michael Moore
- "'Quality Time'—a term invented by businesspeople to justify the lack of time they spend with their kids." Brett Wilson, *Dragon's Den*
- "What was the promise life made to itself the day you were born?" Dawna Markova
- "Secrets of great story are the secrets of the human mind." James Bonnet, *Stealing Fire from the Gods*
- "Commit to the Lord whatever you do, and your plans will succeed." Proverbs 16:3
- "Simplicity is the ultimate sophistication." Leonardo Da Vinci
- "Potential unexpressed turns to pain." Robin Sharma, *The Greatness Guide*

Business and Leadership

Much of what I read is business related. There are many great business ideas, but these ones were the ones that made it to the canvas.

- "Leadership is more than a role; it is a responsibility." Lee Cockerell, *Creating Magic: Ten Common Sense Leadership Strategies from a Life at Disney*
- 4 Most Important words in Management: "What Do You Think?" Tom Peters, *The Little Big Things – 163 Ways to Pursue Excellence*
- "You can't cross a chasm in two jumps." Mark Maybank
- "Leadership — The art of helping people do things they didn't know they could do till they did them." Doug Keeley
- "'SIB-KIS' See It Big! Keep It Simple!" Charlie "Tremendous" Jones, *Life Is Tremendous*
- "Success is the result of the delicate balance between making things happen and letting them happen." Robin Sharma, *The Greatness Guide 2*

Philosophy

Finally, here are a number of ideas of philosophy from a variety of sources. They might not be considered philosophy in the traditional sense, but each one adds something to our understanding of ourselves. I hope you like these.

- "Write and publish your ideas, your thoughts and your philosophy." Jeffrey Gitomer, *Little Teal Book of Trust*

- "Beyond your body, mind and intellect lies your real self ... Discover it!" Swamiji Parthasarathy
- "The human condition is like a man shot with an arrow: painful and urgent." Buddha
- "The two most powerful words: 'I AM'" Rhonda Byrne, *The Secret*
- "Even this shall pass away."
- "We are here to love God and enjoy life." St. Augustine
- Knowledge leads to wisdom which leads to enlightenment
- "The only easy day was yesterday." US Navy SEALs motto
- The goal of life is not happiness, but meaning

You have made it through 133 somewhat random thoughts that filled the Idea Canvas. To quote Landy Chase, a sales trainer I have seen many times, "It's not what you know; it's what you *do* with what you know." I hope that in reviewing some of these ideas, you have found an idea or two (or twenty) that you may want to put into action. Or perhaps you liked the idea of the quote and are going to find the book or author it is from and continue your learning. Whatever you do, do something with what you have learned. You owe it to yourself. To quote one of the authors above, "Therefore, everyone who hears these words of mine *and* puts them into practice is like a wise man who builds his house on the rock." Build your foundation strong through learning *and* action.

The Best Ideas I Ever Took...

I have always considered myself a student and a relatively good one. I constantly worked hard to learn what I needed to learn and to internalize all that I had studied. I want to make myself a better person and found the idea of constant education a natural one. I would consider myself a student of the science of personal development, and this has served me well. And it is all based on advice I took over fifteen years ago.

When I first started at Atlantic Speedy Propane as the General Sales Manager back in the early 1990s, I had never been a sales manager before, let alone considered myself a sales person. I was a marketing product manager, not a salesman! But with this new job, I started studying everything I could on sales and sales management. I was lucky that in addition to becoming exposed early on to Zig Ziglar, I discovered Brian Tracy. My personal development philosophy came directly from him, and I have followed it ever since.

I remember hearing Brian Tracy on one of his audio cassette programs say, "You will be the same tomorrow as you are today, except for the books you read and the people you meet." I really took that message to heart as I started my journey of professional development. Brian also gave me the two best ideas I have ever received, and I have tried to follow them ever since.

The Best Idea I Ever Took: Part 1

The first idea I took and internalized was "Get up twenty minutes earlier every morning and read." The idea was that if you spend twenty minutes every morning reading something that relates to your job, your industry, or your personal development, within a year you will have read fifteen to twenty books. Your peers and competition are not doing this, so within a couple of years, you will have learned more new ideas and become one of the best in your industry. When you read, you take in a few hundred pages what someone has often taken a lifetime of effort and time to develop. And you can get the best of what they have learned quickly and easily.

"I don't have the time to wait twenty-five years to get twenty-five years of experience." By reading books, you bypass all the tons of earth that was required to be mined to get at the ounce of gold, the few nuggets of wisdom that it took others years to learn. You get it for about $20 and a few hours of reading.

"Experience is a great teacher, but the price she extracts is a high one." Through reading, you don't have to spend the years of slogging to get the experience and wisdom it has taken others so much time to learn. Read, study, and you will have this information in a fraction of the time.

But why get up early and read? Why morning? If you wait until the evening, there will always be something coming up, some event or reason that you can't get your reading done. And once you miss a few nights, you get out of the habit and soon you are not doing it. The early morning is quiet, and regardless of how early you start, you can always get up twenty minutes earlier. The ancient sages of India discovered that the prime time your mind is most awake and receptive, the "*sattvik* time," is between 4 a.m. and 6 a.m. Your mind is fresh and alert and you have the best opportunity to focus. Start your day reading positive, uplifting material. Studying also helps set the tone for the day, and it starts you out on a positive footing.

I get up every morning between 4:30 a.m. and 5:00 a.m. and start my morning with reading. Lately I have been reading for up to ninety minutes, and I look forward to that time. I highlight my books, and I have a journal that I take notes in to keep a simple summary of the good ideas I have read. Get up early and read. It is worth it!

The Best Idea I Ever Took: Part 2

The second idea that I have consciously followed for over fifteen years is "Never listen to the radio in your car." Radio is just "bubble gum for the ears," and with all the driving that people do today, this is wasted time. Instead, you should be listening to motivational, inspirational, and educational material that will make you a better person. The idea of a "university on wheels" is a powerful one, and many public libraries have a wide selection of literature on CD. Over the years, I have developed a personal development library of close to two hundred different audio programs, ranging from sales and negotiation techniques, leadership ideas, personal and spiritual development to classic literature. I often tell people

I will never know what the weather will be, as I don't listen to the radio in my car. Listening to CDs over and over helps you internalize the information and become better at what you do.

I have been in business all my adult life, so my focus has been a very practical, business-oriented one and I make no excuse for that. If you want to be the best you can possibly be, you owe it to yourself to take these two ideas to heart. I consider myself Alex Pettes Inc., a personal services corporation dedicated to maximizing the income and potential of Alex Pettes. I am committed to investing in my own business (myself and my personal development) regardless of whether my employer or someone else is doing it. If you wait for someone else to give you training, send you on a course, or give you the time for personal development, you will be waiting a long time. Who cares more about you than you? If you don't think the investment is worth it, neither will anyone else.

"But isn't that a lot of work?" It certainly is effort, but if you have the desire to be the best you can possibly be and excel in your personal development, it is an easy price to pay. "The quality of our life's journey can never be higher than the level of personal development we have attained." Don't get stuck where you are! Take the time to develop yourself and see the personal and professional improvements in your life develop.

I have been actively sharing this advice for many years. I am still amazed at how few people actually take it to heart. I am where I am today due in great measure to the fact that I took this advice faithfully and have tried to follow it. I have an MBA, but I can honestly say I have learned more from the books and tapes over the years that I ever did in my MBA program. Please believe me, it works!

If after all I have tried to share and "sell" you on the importance of reading and listening for your personal development, you still think it is too much work and not worth it, then don't worry about it. Don't do it. You can remain mediocre just like everyone else.

If you are not for a mediocre existence, take my advice. Get up early and read. Turn off the radio and listen to a good CD (or podcast.) You will be better off for doing it.

Put Your Own Oxygen Mask on First

In the previous chapter, I talked about the importance of personal development. As I started to read widely, I met two other authors who had a major influence on me. These were Zig Ziglar and Anthony Robbins. It is hard to describe what Zig gave to me, or who I would be if I had not been influenced by him. My positive, enthusiastic, "super good" attitude was taken directly from him. The body of my personal mission statement ("having everything in life I want if I will just help enough other people get what they want") is a direct take off from Zig's philosophy. Plus, because of one of Zig's sales tapes, I recommitted myself to my personal faith and rededicated myself as a Christian. And that is the eternal gift I can never repay.

From Tony Robbins, the germ of the idea to "create your own unique identity and consistently reinforce it" has manifested into the Cmdr Pettes persona and much of my personal self-talk. His *Personal Power* tapes, which I listened to over thirty days in November 1992, continue to shape who I have become. To all these men and many more, I am grateful.

So over the years, I have practiced and preached these philosophies of ongoing personal and professional development to all who would listen. They have served me well and I want to share so others can get all that I have been privileged to learn. So it was getting somewhat disconcerting to me that in September 2009, I began to think that this focus on my personal development was a selfish undertaking.

I was at a conference, "Connecting for Change," a smaller conference inside the Vancouver Peace Summit. The Vancouver Peace Summit featured a number of Nobel Peace Prize recipients, including His Holiness, the Dalai Lama. The "C4C" conference was a collection of about one hundred and thirty individuals from around the world who are doing amazing things for others in various charitable and social activist endeavours. The idea was to connect them with each other and businesspeople and see what connections could be made for the betterment of all.

One of the exercises we were asked to do was to write down what our personal passion was. This was to be put on a list with all the other attendees so that you could see what passion others had and help facilitate connections with them. I wrote that my passion was the path to self-discovery so that I could be the best I could be and thus better serve others in the future. In my journal the next morning, I reflected on this choice of passion. I wrote, "I feel that this might be too shallow and ego-centric compared to the others here who are so deeply involved in 'other-focused' charities." This really began to bother me. I had been repeating (and believing) my mission statement of "continually contributing in the service to others," and I was now doubting that I was really doing that. If my personal passion was my own personal development, how selfish was that? Was I really this self-centered, shallow person? The idea of that was disconcerting. So I started to be aware of this, and I began to journal and contemplate whether this journey to personal development and self-discovery really was selfish. Amazingly the answer came to me in many different ways from many different people within a period of fewer than thirty days.

The answer was what I termed the *put your own oxygen mask on first* concept. Every time you fly in a plane, as part of the safety demonstrations, the flight attendants show the oxygen mask dropping from the ceiling. You are to pull the mask down, put it over your mouth and nose, breathe normally, and the oxygen will start to flow. Then you are to assist others putting their oxygen masks on, but you must put your own oxygen mask on first. If you don't have your own mask on, you will soon be weak and unable to help anyone else. In fact, you will have gone from helping to hurting, as now you need to be taken care of by others who could be helping those who really need assistance. Let's follow the oxygen mask analogy closely for a minute and see what it tells us.

The plane is flying along normally and then some problems arise. The Captain, who is concerned for your safety, takes action to have the oxygen masks fall from the ceiling. He wants you to be safe; he cares about your safety, but he also cares about the safety of all the other passengers and the plane itself. So he gives you the chance to help yourself. You have to take the action of physically reaching up and pulling down the mask, thus releasing the flow of the life-giving oxygen. Now you have to actually put the mask on over your mouth and nose and adjust the straps so that it fits you. The mask is designed to fit all people, but you make it fit you just right. Now you can breathe normally, as the problem of your not having oxygen is taken care of. Don't worry about the plane—the Captain has that taken care of. Your next task is to help those around you get their own masks on, and get the life giving oxygen flowing for them as it is for you.

First, what is oxygen? It is an absolute requirement for life. You can live for weeks without food, days without water, but only minutes without oxygen. Oxygen is the fuel for our cells to live and thrive. Oxygen is life itself. You need oxygen, and the Captain (or God, or Life, or the Universe, or however you relate to the higher powers) knows this. He wants you to have all the oxygen you need. He has dropped all you need right in front of you. You simply have to take action. *You* must reach up, grab the mask, and put in on. *You* must adjust the mask fit it to your face. The Captain wants you to get this life-giving oxygen, and he has taken steps to put it right in front of you where you are. All you have to do is grab it, put it on and let the life-giving oxygen fill you. Now that you have your connection to Life, your responsibility is to help the others around you do the same.

This analogy really hit me and convinced me that the responsibility to find our individual paths to self-discovery and personal development and take care of ourselves first was the very best thing we could do for other people. If you care about others, truly want to serve them and do good for them, take care of yourself first. The Universe knows this and provides the way for all of us to learn and develop. It puts people and experiences right in front of us all. And I am not the only one who believes this. As I considered this, numerous others reinforced my belief.

The Dalai Lama says the first responsibility we have to others is to start with ourselves. Fix yourself first, then expand the circle to your family, then your community, then your world.

Matthieu Ricard, a French Buddhist monk on the same panel as the Dali Lama at the Vancouver Peace Summit, said it very well. "You can't build a garden with withered flowers. You must start your development within."

James Hollis, a psychologist and author of *Finding Meaning in the Second Half of Life*, says, "A parent's first task is personal growth allied with the conscious assumption of responsibility for the growth of others." As a Dad, this had a powerful impact on me.

He had another quote that I found very significant: "The quality of our life's journey can never be higher than the level of personal development we have attained." Personal development is the key to a better quality of life!

The US Marine Corps Leadership program is founded on eleven principles and fourteen traits they instil into their leaders. The first principle is "Know yourself and seek self-improvement." The Marines have institutionalized leadership development for generations.

General (Ret) Tony Zinni (USMC) wrote the following in his book *Leading the Charge: Leadership Lessons from the Battlefield to the Boardroom*: "If I had to pick a single indicator of a future top leader, I would say it's the degree of his commitment and determination to improve himself, on his own."

The Bhagavad-Gita, the Hindu Scripture, says, "You must raise yourself by yourself."

Finally, one of the moderators at the Connecting for Change conference was Dawna Markova. As I read her book, *I Will Not Die an Unlived Life,* after the conference, I found this quote from one of her mentors, Parker Palmer: "Self care is never a selfish act—it is simply good stewardship of the only gift I have; the gift I was put on earth to offer to others."

So, all these items coming into my path confirmed that my journey of spiritual and personal development was exactly the thing I needed to be doing. I felt not only validated but satisfied. I honestly believe I want to serve others, as this service is really what we are all called to do. And this focus on personal development was not only going to help me achieve this lofty service goal, but it was also self-reinforcing. I was getting the benefit of living a more full life, increasing my chances at leadership and significance, and making my life more clear and positive along the way! I have my own oxygen mask firmly on, and I will continue to breathe deeply—for my own benefit and that of others.

Even This Shall Pass Away:
Enjoy All of Life's Fleeting Moments

In February 2009, I had the opportunity to spend a week in India studying ancient Vedanta philosophies with a wonderful eighty-two-year-old swami, Swami Parthasarathy. This man started The Vedanta Institute, a school where students spend three years, 365 days a year, learning these ancient wisdom philosophies. Swami means teacher, and this teacher was especially well loved and was given the more familiar term of respect, *Swamiji*. While Swamiji certainly was a Hindu, and also taught from the Hindu religious text the Bhagavad-Gita, his primary focus was showing how Vedanta wisdom appeared throughout all cultures and applied to all people.

As we went through the course, there were studies of the ancient Vedantic life philosophies that had been learned and passed down for over five thousand years. In addition to that, Swamiji had written three books that the students studied. The first was called *The Fall of the Human Intellect*. The second, interestingly, was *Selected English Literature*. Swamiji had taken a number of English poems and passages from famous literature and combined them into a single book along with his commentary of each one. Students spent time reading and discussing these poems. One that had a great impact on me was a classic poem by Theodore Tilton called "Even This Shall Pass Away," also known by the title "The King's Ring."

As the author repeated in the last line of every stanza, the idea that "even this shall pass away" on first reading seemed quite a gloomy and depressing idea. The King, who is the primary focus of the poem, has all kinds of things happen to him, mostly good, and for him to keep repeating that they will be no longer seemed to be a negative message. In fact, I believe the poem has a strong positive message when you examine it closely. Here is the poem.

Even This Shall Pass Away

Once in Persia reigned a King,
Who upon his signet ring,
Graved a maxim true and wise,
Which, if held before his eyes,
Gave him counsel at a glance,
Fit for every change or chance.
Solemn words and these are they;
"Even This Shall Pass Away."

Trains of camels through the sand,
Brought him gems from Samarkand;
Fleets of galleys through the seas
Brought him pearls to match with these;
But he counted not his gain,
Treasures of the mine or main;
"What is Wealth?" the king would say;
"Even This Shall Pass Away"

Mid the revels of his court,
At the zenith of his sport,
When the palms of all his guests
Burned with clapping at his jests.
He, amid his figs and wine,
Cried, "Oh loving friends of mine!
Pleasures come, but not to stay.
'Even This Shall Pass Away.'"

Lady, fairest ever seen,
Was the bride he crowned his queen.
Pillowed on his marriage bed,
Softly to his soul he said:
"Though no bridegroom ever pressed
Fairer bosom to his breast,
Mortal flesh must come to clay -
Even This Shall Pass Away."

Fighting on a furious field,
Once a javelin pierced his shield;
Soldiers, with a loud lament,
Bore him bleeding to his tent.
Groaning from his tortured side,
"Pain is hard to bear!" he cried;
"But with patience, day by day,
Even This Shall Pass Away."

Towering in the public square,
Twenty cubits in the air,
Rose his statue, carved in stone.
Then the King, disguised, unknown,

Stood before his sculptured name,
Musing meekly: "What is fame?
Fame is but a slow decay;
Even This Shall Pass Away."

Struck with palsy, sore and old,
Waiting at the Gates of Gold,
Said he with his dying breath,
"Life is done, but what is Death?"
Then, in answer to the King,
Fell a sunbeam on his ring,
Showing by a heavenly ray,
"Even This Shall Pass Away."

Theodore Tilton

At first glance, it does appear to be somewhat negative. The King has all this wealth and says, "Oh well, it will all be gone one day." He is at the top of his sport, surrounded by friends who love him, great food and drink, and he says, "Pleasures come but not to stay, even this shall pass away." Does he not want to enjoy all these good gifts? The pleasures of life?

Then with the most beautiful woman ever seen, who is now his wife, he is thinking, "Mortal flesh must come to clay?" Even the love of his life will one day be taken from him and this is a positive thing?

The stanza describing his wounding in battle, (when the King with stoic posture says he will with patience, day by day, endure this pain), begins to endear him to the reader. And his humility about his great fame as he stares at his statue towering over the public square might make us think that this is a good and righteous posture.

But as I read the final stanza, a number of thoughts come to mind. He is sick and dying and in his anguish cries out to heaven, which answers him. We all want to know that our time on Earth will continue into the afterlife, and so do we look at this passage with a quasi-religious overtone? After all, it was a "heavenly ray" that answered the King. (Not that there is anything wrong with our thoughts and beliefs about heaven, as I certainly don't think so.) But there is more. Here is what I think the poem is trying to say, and why it so moved me.

The message of this poem is to realize that all the things we have, or possess, or are, or will be, are fleeting. And that is not a bad thing. It is a real, true fact of life. And nothing you can do will change this reality. No matter what we accumulate, what experiences we enjoy or dread—that which brings us great pleasure or pain, that which we can control or that which just happens to us for no known reason—even this shall pass away. So realize that the life we have and the pleasures (and pain) we have are fleeting, and be thankful for what they bring to us. Be in the moment of these things and learn and take from them what you can, as they will not be here forever. This is one of the great lessons of this simple yet deep poem.

This poem also tells us that our identity is not the temporary things we are experiencing, and that we should not tie our personal self-worth to whom or what we have at the moment. We may have riches and power, but we are not rich and powerful, as even this shall pass away. We may have great achievement and fame, but we are not champions and famous forever, as even this shall pass away. We may be of ill health and weak, but we are not sickly, as even this shall pass away.

I was so moved by this poem that when I came back from India in March 2009 I had my own ring made engraved with the phrase, "Even This Shall Pass Away." I have worn it ever since, as a reminder to myself, that whatever I have, be, or do will not be forever. It reminds me to enjoy the moments of pleasure and success as they come and to savour them. It reminds me when I get angry or upset at something that even this shall pass away, and not to get so upset about it. It is a public declaration of my journey to be a more positive, appreciative, and understanding person, and it catches me when I am not those things. I am not perfect—just ask my wife! I am consciously trying to make the effort to be a better person, and this is just one of the "tools" that helps me along the way.

As I was researching this poem on the Internet after returning from India, I discovered that there is a well-known similar phrase of Jewish origin. That phrase is "This too shall pass." This similarity speaks to the fact that wisdom of the ages is ageless and that no one holds the copyright on philosophies that help people. If you are like me, you have rarely spent time reading and dissecting poetry since you were forced to back in high school. I spent well over a month reading and journaling and trying to understand the thirty or so poems that the Swamiji combined in this little book of poetry. I am no master teacher. I am just one who has found a little wisdom and wants to share it.

It is interesting as I end this chapter to ponder if true wisdom falls subject to the phase "Even This Shall Pas Away." Perhaps it is the one thing that does not pass away so that the next person or generation can discover it for themselves anew and find the joy in its discovery. Hmmm...

Lessons on the Wing

It is funny how when you have your eyes open and your mind is tuned to receive that you discover things along your path. This is the whole idea behind the thought, "When the student is ready, the teacher will appear." I find it interesting that a number of the teachers that have appeared to me have had wings.

When I was India, I spent a week studying philosophy and the meaning of life with an eighty-two-year-old teacher, Swamiji Parthasarathy. This swami was not a religious teacher; instead, he taught the ancient Vedanta philosophies of personal development and spiritual enlightenment. In his first book, *The Fall of the Human Intellect*, he talks about the "wonderful equipment" man has been given, namely the Mind and the Intellect. These are to serve him, but too often we don't understand what they are and end up spending our lives in service to them. Especially the Mind.

So what is the difference between the "Mind" and the "Intellect?" Is this not just semantics? Different ways of saying the same thing? According to the ancient Vedanta teachings they are not. So what is the distinction?

The Mind is where we have our emotions, feelings, impulses, likes, and dislikes. The Intellect is where we have our thinking, reasoning, judging, and deciding. The Mind's emotions and desires are insatiable; they can never be satisfied. We constantly are having images put into our Mind that create our desires. The Mind constantly wants things to acquire and enjoy. The problem is that upon the acquisition or enjoyment of an object or being, the desire wanes and we find that we are still searching for more items to acquire and enjoy. The Mind tells us that Happiness is found in the external world, so we need to continually find more things to acquire and enjoy. The Mind is like a fire that never will stop burning until all the fuel is consumed or it is extinguished. That is why we need our Intellect.

The Intellect is the part of our brain that gives the meaning to the object and items we want to acquire and enjoy and moderates our desires. Desires are not the issue; it is the uncontrolled desires that are! We need our Intellect to discern what it is that we should desire in the first place. Otherwise the mind cannot control itself, and we find ourselves out of control. Just because we can perceive something does not mean we should have it.

This idea was further discussed in the Swamiji's second book, *Selected English Poems*. One of the poems, "The Pineapple and The Bee," by William Cowper, described in a simple way man's uncontrolled desires and their consequences. Interesting how over the years it was the poets who really studied the emotions and nature of man. And often they hid these subtle messages in their wonderful words, allowing the reader to discover these ideas and truths anew for themselves. Here is the poem.

The Pineapple and the Bee

The pineapples in triple row,
Were basking hot and all in blow,
A bee of most discerning taste
Perciev'd the fragrance as he pass'd,
On eager wing the spoiler came,
And search'd for crannies in the frame,
Urg'd his attempt on ev'ry side,
To ev'ry pane his trunk applied,
But still in vain, the frame was tight
And only pervious to the light.
Thus having wasted half the day,
He trimmed his flight another way.

Methinks, I said, in thee I find
The sin and madness of mankind;
To joys forbidden man aspires,
Consumes his soul with vain desires;
Folly the spring of his pursuit,
And disappointment all the fruit.
While Cynthio ogles as she passes
The nymph between two chariot glasses,
She is the pineapple, and he
The silly unsuccessful bee.
The maid who views with pensive air
The show-glass fraught with glitt'ring ware,
Sees watches, bracelets, rings and lockets,
But sighs at thought of empty pockets,
Like thine her appetite is keen,
But ah the cruel glass between!

Our dear delights are often such,
Expos'd to view but not to touch;
The sight our foolish heart inflames,
We long for pineapples in frames,
With hopeless wish one looks and lingers,
One breaks the glass and cuts his fingers,
But they whom truth and wisdom lead,
Can gather honey from a weed.

William Cowper

The Bee is likened to man. It perceives the pineapple and the Mind tells it that it must have it. It spends half a day looking in vain to find a crack in the glass where it can get in, the "crannies in the frame." It fails and flies away, having wasted a significant amount of its short life. Our Mind, when unchecked by the discernment of the Intellect, is like the bee. "To joys forbidden man aspires which consume his soul with vain desires." We see items and like the maid, we desire "watches, bracelets, rings and lockets," and get upset with ourselves and life at the "thought of empty pockets."

As the poem continues, we often get upset and consume half our lives "longing for pineapples in frames," for things that are not needed. Or we become rash, breaking the glass and cutting our fingers in the process. But if you consciously use your Intellect you can find joy where it is, where you are. I love the last lines, which say, "But they whom truth and wisdom lead can gather honey from a weed." I have found this simple poem about a little bee very helpful in my personal life. Is what I think I desire what I really want? My Mind is insatiable and always wanting more, and it tells me to go get more and more. And when I do, it is not happy and still wants more. By making conscious efforts to use my discerning Intellect, I am learning to find happiness and joy within myself, not in the objects and items I can buy or enjoy. It is not easy, and I am certainly not perfect, but by giving these thoughts conscious review, I am making progress toward being a person I more want to be. What kind of person is that? A person who has less anxiety about material possessions and the need to get more and more. "I *will* have everything in life I want *if* I can just help enough other people get what they want." And in most cases, what people really, truly want, is not more stuff. Thank you, little bee, for this lesson.

My second little winged instructor is the hummingbird. Here is a simple little story I heard that made a big impact on me.

The forest was on fire! All the animals were scared and running away from the devastation that fire can cause. As they all stood outside the forest in the safety of the clearing, they noticed that the hummingbird was busy going back and forth into the raging forest fire. They noticed that the little hummingbird was flying to the stream, getting a small drop of water in his beak (as hummingbirds are so small and can't carry much) and flying into the forest. The hummingbird would drop the water on the fire and come back out for more water. Over and over. Without stopping and without making much of an impact on the raging fire from what all the animals could see.

The other animals began to laugh at the hummingbird, wasting all his time and energy and not even having an impact. They stopped the hummingbird and asked him why he continued to fly in and out of the fire as all his work was not making a visible difference. The hummingbird humbly replied, "Because I am doing all I can."

I heard this story first at the Vancouver Connecting for Change conference in September 2009. The simple story affected me greatly. Contribute even a very little bit is still contributing. Sometimes it is easy to be overwhelmed by the large magnitude of problems facing us and the world today. Poverty. Hunger. Global Warming. Diseases. Huge, seemingly unsolvable problems. Not to mention our own personal problems and those of our family. They often seem as big and unsolvable! The hummingbird story was a challenge to me to ask myself am I doing all I can? All I can for my family, for my wife and girls? For my immediate and extended family? For my work and my company? For my community? And even for myself?

As I pondered this simple message, I realized that we have no idea what our efforts will produce or the impact they will have. There are many such stories of how small things grow into great things. And even if they don't turn into world-changing effects, that is not the issue. The moral of the hummingbird story is *not* that by making all these small trips that the hummingbird saved the day, the fire went out and the forest was saved. No, the fire keeps raging; the problems still exist. But that is no excuse for not doing all you can. Who knows what impact our small efforts will produce? Will the small thing you did for a child make a lasting impact on his or her life? Will your actions as a hummingbird inspire the other animals of the forest to start doing something and thus multiply your efforts? Or will just doing your part at least make you feel good, knowing that you did not sit idly by watching the fire? Amazingly, you always get back more than what you give; you just may not relate the two events. It *is* more blessed to give than to receive. Life *is* to give, not to take. I am consciously trying to be the hummingbird in all my areas of life. I may not make a big difference, but I hope that I am at least doing all I can.

I found this hummingbird necklace in Vancouver the night after hearing the story. Coincidence? I doubt it.

Goal Setting: How Can You Hit a Target You Don't Even Have?

Many great books have been written on the subject of goal setting. An organization's mission statement is nothing but the goal of what that company wants to become. It often gets long and protracted, because it tries to answer the needs of all stakeholders. I was first "sold" on the idea of having written goals back in the early 1990s, when I started studying to become a better sales manager and sales person. I read many books and listened to many tapes, and the theme of goal setting as an underlying requirement to ensure success kept coming out. Perhaps the best goal-setting program I ever discovered came from Zig Ziglar. Its simplicity and its idea to set goals in all areas of your life, including the often neglected physical and spiritual aspects of life, was what appealed to me. Zig had a simple multistep formula that I have been following for many years. If you are already taking the time to write goals and feel that this segment may not have much to offer you, I would still encourage you to read, as there may be a twist on things that you may find helpful.

A) *What is it that you want?*

The first step in any goal setting process is to decide what you want to have, be, or do. This is not as easy as it sounds, and the following process will help you get to the core of what it is you really want.

The first step is what I call the Mind Dump. Here is where you take a sheet (or a few sheets) of paper and just spend twenty to thirty minutes writing down all the things that you think you might like to have, be, or do. The purpose is not to judge whether these goals are good or attainable; the key is to write down as much as you can with no filters. If it comes in your mind, write it down. It may stimulate your thoughts to go in another direction or add some related ideas. You will have no trouble at first, but then you will stop and realize you have only written for ten minutes. Push yourself to write as much as you can. If you can go solid for more than thirty minutes, then keep going! The objective is to have as much written down as possible.

To aid in this process, and to make sure that you have a full balance of goals, write the following headings at the top of the page before you begin. These are the seven key areas of life:

Financial – Career – Family – Physical – Spiritual – Friends – Personal

As you are writing, you may find that most of your goals are in a few areas and less in another. By referring to these headings, it will help stimulate your thoughts when you get into a slump.

After you have done this thirty-minute exercise, stop and put these papers away for twenty-four to forty-eight hours. Allow your subconscious mind to percolate these ideas.

B) Filter Your Goals

The next step is to filter your goals. Go back to the laundry list of ideas that you did a day or two earlier. Here are the questions you must ask and answer *yes* to in order to keep this goal on your list. In this way, you make sure that the goals you are going to spend the time to develop in full are the appropriate ones for you. If the answer for any of the items on your list is *no*, cross that item off the list.

First Goal Filter—Must Answer YES to All

1. Is it morally right and fair?
2. Is it consistent with other goals?
3. Can I emotionally commit to finishing this goal?
4. Can I see myself reaching this goal?
5. Is it MY goal?

Once you have gone through this first set of questions or filters, you are able to progress to the second set of questions. These are the Basic Six Desires all people want. If your goal will not help you get these basic desires, they are not worth pursuing, and you must cross it off the list.

Second Goal Filter—The Basic Six Desires

1. Will it make me happier?
2. Will it make me healthier?
3. Will it make me more prosperous?
4. Will it make me more friends?
5. Will it make me more secure?
6. Will it make me have more peace of mind?

C) Sort and Prioritize Your Goals

Now that you have a smaller list of goals that are worth pursuing, you have to sort them into the various areas of your life—that is, to put them into one of the seven categories you listed on the top of the page. For this, I suggest using seven sheets of paper.

Seven Goal Categories

1. Financial
2. Career
3. Family
4. Physical
5. Spiritual
6. Friends
7. Personal

Once you transposed them to the seven sheets of paper, now you must write in the left margin beside them what the time frame is for these goals. Is this something you think you could achieve in a year? Three years? Five years? Ten years? More than ten years? So write a 1, 3, 5, 10, or 10+ beside each goal for each sheet of paper.

D) Prioritize and Pick the Goals for Further Development

Now you are sitting with seven sheets of paper, one for each area of your life, with a list of goals and the timeframes you think you could achieve them in. So far you may be thinking, *This is a lot of work! Is it worth all this time and effort?* It is estimated that less than 1 percent of the population has a series of written goals that they are consciously working towards. A famous study at Yale University asked the graduating class in 1965 what their goals were for the future. Only 3 percent of the class had taken the time to write out their goals. Twenty-five years later, they followed up with the surviving members of this class. Researchers discovered that the 3 percent who had taken the time to write out their goals and a plan for their achievement had a financial net worth greater that the other 97 percent of the class combined! Therefore, if financial achievement is one of your goals, this is a ringing testimonial! If it is not, then you should at least realize the power of having these goals written down along with a plan for their achievement.

Now is the hard part: picking which goals you should focus on. As you go through the list, some of the goals may be very similar, merely stated in different ways. Perhaps there is a chance to combine a few very similar goals. If you have written them down and the same idea appears a number of times, this tells you that this area must be important to you. Once you have spent some time reviewing all the goals, you have to pick the ones that warrant a full, written action plan. Ideally, you should have a few goals from each area of your life to work on; however, practically, I know that having so many targets can be overwhelming. I would pick your top four to six most important, most significant, "if achieved they would make the biggest difference in your life" goals, then prepare to write them out in full.

E) *The Seven-Step Goal Procedure Chart*

Enclosed is a blank Seven-Step Goal Procedure chart you can copy and fill out. The seven steps are designed to help you work through the process of achieving the goal, by making you consciously aware of what you need to do.

1. **Identify your goal**. Write out the goal that you want to achieve.

2. **My benefits from reaching this goal**. Here is where you list all the things that you will achieve when you reach the goal. This is important, as this list will help provide you the motivation you need to help achieve the goal. These are the main reasons you are doing what you are doing anyway! Listing these will help keep you focused on the great reasons you are working so hard.

3. **Major obstacles and mountains to climb to reach this goal**. All worthwhile goals are tough to achieve. They take work and effort. Here is where you list all the things that you need to overcome to achieve your goal. By doing so, you also realize that many of the things you thought were so tough are actually quite manageable when you write them down. And it also helps focus you on the areas you need to work on to accomplish your goal.

4. **Skills or knowledge required to reach this goal**. What do you need to help achieve your goal? If it is physical, do you know how to eat and exercise properly? Do you need to learn some budgeting or financial skills? What is it you don't know that is holding you back? By listing those things here, you can start the plan to find out and get the knowledge and skills you need.

5. **Individuals, groups, companies, and organizations to work with to reach the goal**. Who can help you? List them so you can act on them.

6. **Plan of action to reach this goal**. Here are the real steps you need to act on. List the actions and things you need to do to start on the path to achieving your goal. The time you take to plan out your actions will greatly reduce the time they take and increase the probability that they will be done. This is where the rubber meets the road and you start working!

7. **Completion date**. You must set the end date to accomplish the goal. Goals without deadlines are just dreams. By setting a date, it puts the pressure on you to make sure that you are taking the actions necessary to achieve this time. Be accountable to yourself and set a realistic time to achieve the goal.

General Goals Procedure Chart

GOAL #1   GOAL #2

STEP 1   Identify your Goals

STEP 2   My Benefits from Reaching This Goal

STEP 3   Major Obstacles & Mountains to Climb to Reach this Goal

STEP 4   Skills or Knowledge Required to Reach this Goal

STEP 5 Individuals, Groups, Companies & Organizations to Work with to Reach this goal

STEP 6   Plan of Action to Reach this Goal

STEP 7   Completion Date

F) Get Started!

The above exercise has helped you determine what you really want. You have thought out clearly why you want this and set a plan of action to achieve this! Now just get started! Take the first steps for each goal you said you were going to do and get moving!

There are many simple ways to help you keep motivated. Place Post-It notes with the goal on your bathroom mirror or fridge to remind you what you want to do. Paste a photo of the image that might represent your goal—a slim person, a vacation brochure, the new car you want to get, etc. One of my goals was to get into shape, as I had booked a weekend to train with the US Navy SEALs in October, more than eight months away. When I was training and working out, I wore a rubber wristband that said "Navy" to remind me. I got a new dog tag with the date of the weekend and kept it in my pocket as a reminder to eat properly when I was out.

I would also recommend keeping these goal sheets handy and making a point of reviewing them every week (say, Sunday night when you start planning for your week.) You can review the list of all the things you have to do, congratulate yourself on what you did well, and keep yourself reminded of why you are on the path to achieving this goal.

It is work, and it takes time, but it is truly worth every bit of effort you put in. I made a commitment to personal development and set a goal to read every morning and never listen to the radio, and I have kept that up. I wanted to be President of TFI before I turned forty, and I set a goal to do so when I was thirty-five. On January 27, 2002, I even drew a picture of myself (the power of visualization) on my fortieth birthday sitting at my desk, with a name tag that said

"President," plus photos of my family and the other things I wanted to achieve by the time I was forty. And I am proud to say I became President of TFI on June 30, 2006, four months before my fortieth birthday.

How can you hit a target you don't even have? And as the Cheshire Cat said to Alice, "If you don't know where you want to go, any road will take you there." Invest the time in yourself and set goals in all aspects of your life. You are worth it! Goal setting works.

My visual goal to become President. (Please remember I went to business school, not art school!)

Sales Signs along the Way

I have been in sales management for almost twenty years and have developed a number of best practices and ideas that I have shared with many other sales managers. I enjoy sharing my ideas, and I hope that you like this simple yet effective one. One of the ideas that I developed over fifteen years ago was to have a series of signs hanging in the room during sales meetings. I cannot remember where I got the idea from, so I will just take the credit for implementing and using it.

These signs are made of a corrugated plastic and are approximately 3' X 3'. I had a number of motivational and sales messages printed on them that I would refer to during the course of the meeting. The concept was to have a bunch of visible, positive sales ideas that we could refer to during the sales meeting. If the salespeople at the meeting were not listening to me, at least they could be reading some positive messages so they could get something out of the meeting!

I have taken the ideas on the signs from a number of sources, and at every meeting I continue to put them up. Repetition is the mother of skill and the sales staff at TFI will tell you that they have gotten to know these signs and the messages quite well over the past ten years!

I have listed the signs below, along with some commentary. If there is one or more of these that you like, please feel free to copy and use it, as I have taken all the ideas from others. Reading and understanding these "signs along the way" may also help you better serve your customers and become a more professional salesperson. Everyone sells, and everyone is in sales. Your title may not be "Salesperson," but as we all interact and try to influence others, learning a few sales lessons is always a good idea.

Nothing happens until somebody sells something

I have a brass ship's bell mounted beside my desk with the above phrase engraved on a small plaque. It is rung whenever one of our sales staff gets a new customer or big order. It reminds us that until an organization sells something to somebody, nothing else matters or happens. All companies and organizations exist to serve others, and a sale is a direct expression that the other person has chosen us to serve their needs. This is to be celebrated and appreciated.

Spectacular achievement is always preceded by unspectacular preparation

There is nothing exciting or glamorous in the preparations we make. Athletes practice, train, and drill so that their performance gets the result. I like this sign, as it says that to make a spectacular achievement, you *always* have to do the hard prep work first.

> **"You can have everything in life you want**
> **if you will just help enough other people**
> **get what they want." Zig Ziglar**

This is Zig Ziglar's often-repeated statement that I augmented and modified for myself. He is famous for this phrase.

> **Results = Activity x Effectiveness**

I call this formula the "Secret Success Formula." You can't manage results; you can only manage activity. Results are the by-products of activities. But most people just focus on the results. This is backwards, and the formula reminds us of this. So to get the results you desire, you must (a) increase your activity levels, (b) get more effective at what you do, and ideally (c) do both together! This is true in all areas of our lives, but especially in sales.

> **5 Reasons People Don't Buy**
> - **No Money**
> - **No Need**
> - **No Hurry**
> - **No Desire**
> - **No Trust**

If someone does not buy from you, there are only five reasons why. Professional salespeople must have a plan to work on each of these five reasons. The one reason customers will never tell you about and the one that is the most important is trust. The rest can be overcome. Lack of trust by the customer toward the salesperson is often invisible and very difficult to repair if it is damaged. Guard your integrity and be trustworthy.

The Only Three Ways to Increase Sales:
- **Increase the number of new customers**
- **Increase the frequency of customer purchase**
- **Increase the amount of each purchase**

This is a universal truth that applies to all businesses of all types. This simple wisdom is often overlooked and not considered. A great business should have plans and strategies to grow their business consciously in each of the three areas. I have never found a business that this simple formula does not apply toward. Ignore it at your peril.

Your Attitude, not your Aptitude,
determines your Altitude

A great and simple phrase that proves that hard work, determination, and a positive outlook will get you far.

To increase the number of your successes, you have to increase the number of your failures

---

This is from Thomas Watson, founder of IBM. Don't be afraid to try stuff. You are just closer to something that works!

> **Selling Cycle Stages**
> **Prospecting > Qualification > Set Appointment >**
> **Presentation > Handling Objections > Closing >**
> **Product Delivery > Follow-up/Generating Referrals**

Very few sales professionals know the eight consecutive stages of the selling cycle. You need to have a conscious plan for every stage if you are to be the most effective you can be. Ignore any one or more of these stages at your peril.

> **Your raise will become effective as soon as you are**

I often get comments about this one. True long-term success and growth only comes with effectiveness. Time and tenure just mask the reality that business pays for performance and sales is the most visible display of this truth.

> **What did you do today to increase your personal and**
> **professional effectiveness?**

Growth and development is a constant, never-ending process. Focus on making yourself better every day.

> **Selling Isn't Telling. It's Asking.**

A simple yet often not followed truth of sales. Ask and listen to what customers need and desire.

> **80% of all sales are made after the 5th closing attempt**

This describes that most salespeople give up the process too early. Customer buying cycles have become longer and more involved, so stick with it and keep adding value for your customer. Be persistent!

> **The most important part of the sales process is ...**
> **PROSPECTING**

Until you have someone to talk to, nothing else matters. All professional long-term salespeople know and understand this. Getting the order or "closing" gets all the glamour and attention, but the best people know that prospecting is the most important step in a long, successful sales career. Not insignificantly, it is the first of the eight steps in the selling process.

> **The Sales Person Is the "Pointy End of the Spear"**

In the air force, they call the fighter pilots the "pointy end of the spear." It is the point of the organization that encounters the enemy. But if the shaft of the spear is not aligned behind the pointy end, you have no effectiveness. I like this phrase, as it describes how the sales person is the primary point of contact of the company with the customer. But this is all in vain if the rest of the organization is not aligned behind and supporting the salesperson and their service to the customer. Sales may get the glamour, but the rest of the company is who really gets the job done in the long term for the customer.

Business is not War. It's Combat.

Continuing with the fighter pilot analogy, I like this expression, as it personalizes the responsibilities of the salesperson. Countries and companies wage war. Individual pilots and salespeople engage in combat. In combat between two competing salespeople, someone wins and someone loses. Someone gets the order, and someone does not. This phrase focuses the responsibility on the individual salesperson for their results and makes them accountable. No blaming the big, bad company. *You* are responsible!

The CUSTOMER is the big winner in any sales transaction.

This is a truism I learned from Zig Ziglar. While the salesperson and the company may make a small profit when a sale is made, it is the customer who enjoys the benefits of the product purchased, often for years to come. The profit the salesperson makes is often spent before it is made! The customer is the big, long-term winner from the sales transaction, and this phrase reminds the salesperson to remain focused on doing what is best for the customer, as the customer is the true winner!

Keep Pumping!

See the chapter "Lessons of the Pump." Don't give up!

> ## It is 1/6ᵗʰ as expensive to sell to an existing customer versus selling a new customer

Keep your existing customers happy. They already know and like you enough to have bought from you once. Don't take them for granted and keep servicing them. It is in the salesperson's best interest to keep existing customers happy and buying from them.

> ## If you Plan to Win and Prepare to Win, you can Expect to Win

Another life truism about preparation, goal setting, and persistence. Do all these things, and you can truly expect success because you have prepared and planned for it.

> ## People don't buy what it is. They buy what it does.

This phrase reminds salespeople to focus on the true benefit customers receive when they purchase your product or service. In my business, customers don't want a large stainless steel machine; they want the ice cream, slush or fried chicken the machine makes for them. They don't want belts and motors and pulleys. They want the profits that selling the products our machines make brings them. That is what customers really buy.

Persistence Pays

Keep Pumping and never give up! It pays results!

If you don't ask, people can't say YES!

This is a reminder for salespeople to always ask for the business. If you don't ask, how can the customer say YES! Don't be afraid they will say NO. Ask and expect a YES!

Selling is transference of Feeling

This is a great one from Zig that reminds salespeople to get customers emotionally involved and excited about owning the product. All buying decisions are made emotionally and justified logically. Get the customer to feel excited about the purchase and you will have a better chance to serve them.

"If I had 8 hours to cut a cord of wood, I would spend the first 3 hours sharpening my axe." Abraham Lincoln

Last but not least is this great quote. This is the same concept as Steven Covey's seventh habit, "Sharpen the Saw." It challenges us to take the time to develop ourselves and our capabilities. To make ourselves more effective and keep from getting worn out and dull. You can cut more wood with less effort with a sharp axe. I love the quote, because it also challenges us to take a great deal of time to work on ourselves. Abe did not say take five minutes out of eight hours to get the axe better; he said *three hours*. Working on yourself is the best investment you can make for your career, your family, and your customers.

The Cmdr's Perspective on Sales Management

My journey into the world of sales management was a bit unusual in that I never really started out in sales. Most sales managers start in sales, then, due to their achievement, tenure, or desire to progress, end up becoming sales managers. While this is the normal way to develop sales managers, allow me to raise a note of caution. A great salesperson will not necessarily become great sales manager. The skills are different, and what made the person successful in sales will not necessarily make that person a successful sales manager (or any manager, for that matter.) With that caveat, allow me to give my perspectives on sales management from an almost twenty-year career.

As I mentioned, I became the General Sales Manager for Atlantic Speedy Propane from my role as a marketing product manager. Suddenly I had approximately thirty-five salespeople reporting to me, and I had never been in sales or really managed people for that matter! There are numerous books on sales management, and entire university courses devoted to the subject, so what will follow are some tidbits and ideas that have served me over my career. I hope they give you some good ideas to help you.

So, what is effective sales management? The goal of the sales manager is to achieve the sales objectives. Period. That is the primary reason to have a sales manager. How do you do that? In my opinion, the role of the sales manager is as follows:

Role of the Sales Manager

A sales manager must create an environment that allows salespeople to motivate themselves. To do this they must provide three things:

a. **Leadership**. Lead from the front, lead by example, servant leadership, remove barriers and obstacles to achievement.

b. **Coaching**. "A planned process of assistance designed to aid the person in the achievement of their goals."

c. **Training**. Product training, sales training.

The sales manager's role is to build, train and develop their team into an effective selling force. I like the definitions of the 3 things the sales manager has to use at their disposal.

Leadership: Many books have been written on leadership, but my personal favourite model of leadership is that of *servant leadership*. This is not a command-and-control style but one of a helpful servant, focused on making sure the needs of the team are addressed. Not slave leadership, as the leader who does what the team tells him to do, but a firm and helpful leader who, being focused on the real needs of his team, does all he can to aid his staff toward their individual as well as their collective goals.

Coaching: I love this definition of coaching, especially when you break down each element of the definition. *Planned* assumes a logical multistep, thought-out approach. *Process* indicates the various stages that the person goes through. *Assistance* implies support and guidance, not doing the work. *Achievement of their goals* focuses on the fact that goals have been developed and set and thus a planned target is created. Coaching is a planned process, not a random collection of activities. All the best performers (athletes, singers, actors, and even businesspeople) have a coach. Coaching is one of the most underutilized concepts in business.

Training: These are the skills needed to get the job done. Skills can be learned, so they must be taught.

Now that we have a definition of what sales management should be, here are a few specific ideas on how to become better sales manager (or really any manager).

1. Feed Your Eagles, Starve Your Turkeys

Eagles are the high performers who command respect and achieve the results. Eagles hunt in a wide area and find the new opportunities and business. Eagles hard at work make the task look effortless as they soar from opportunity to opportunity. Eagles also have wings and can fly away as they have many options open to them, so your job is to keep your eagles happy and on your team.

Turkeys are the low performers who spend most of their time on the ground, scratching in the dirt for whatever small morsels of business are already there. Turkeys get stuck in the coop and have few options. They spend most of their time hoping that the farmer (or sales manager) does not focus on them and have them for dinner!

So what is a sales manager to do? My perspective is that effective sales managers spend 80 percent of their time focusing on their eagles, and only 20 percent of their time focusing on the turkeys. In reality, the opposite is often the case. Sales managers often focus the majority of their time on the struggling performers, hoping to get their performance up a few percentage points or trying to get them to at least achieve their quotas. Real sales professionals know quotas are just minimum expectations, not the ultimate goal.

Break this mould and spend the majority of your time on your eagles. Help them to double, triple or quadruple their targets. How do you do this and still spend time with the turkeys, as they may not be turkeys at all, but developing baby eaglets. The easy answer is to spend one-on-one time with your eagles and spend group time with your turkeys.

Eagles are the high performers. They welcome the coaching and attention as they always are striving to get better. Invest your time and energy where you can get the most results, and that is with the eagles. Help the turkeys to develop into eagles, and if they can't, get rid of the turkeys and find some eagles, or at least baby eaglets.

2. You Can't Manage Results, Only Activity

Here are a few concepts to consider as you focus your efforts on managing activities rather than the results. Results are the product of the activities being done, so while it is easy to focus on results (sales goals, number of deals, invoicing, etc.), the best sales managers focus their teams to get their activities done and done well.

a. **The Secret Success Formula:
Results = Activity x Effectiveness**
To increase your results, you have to

i. Increase the level of activity: work harder (make more sales calls)
ii. Increase the level of effectiveness: work better (close deals with less calls)
iii. Increase both: work smarter!

Thomas Watson, founder of IBM, said, "To double your success, you have to double your failures." While it is easy to see the results of the sales person's efforts, these results are the by-product of activities they are doing. Just having the sales person make more calls and do more work (increase activity) will increase results. But there are only so many more calls you can make until you hit the limit. Spend your time as a sales manager monitoring the number of calls your staff make. Monitor how many calls it takes them to close the sale, and work on the steps to help them close the deals with less effort. This is the harder part of sales management, but if you want to be the best, this is the only way to do it.

b. The Only Three Ways to Grow Any Business

In any business, there are only three basic ways to grow sales. You need to have a conscious plan for each one and make your sales staff focus their activities on each one. I have never found a business where these three steps did not apply. This is a simple yet very powerful idea.

i. Increase the number of customers
ii. Increase the customer's frequency of purchase
iii. Increase the customer's amount per purchase

Often sales staff focus their efforts on the first item, getting more new customers. The sales gurus would say that it costs six times as much to get a new customer (time and effort) as it does to keep an existing customer, yet the focus on new customers is where virtually all businesses and sales staff spend the majority of their time. As a manager, make sure your staff also spend their time on the other two ways (monitoring those activities), and you will see dramatic results.

Sales managers are held accountable to senior management for results. However, merely focusing on those results is not the way to get them. You must spend your time planning, monitoring, and improving your team's activity and effectiveness. As your activity and effectiveness grow, according to the Secret Success Formula, your results will grow and will continue to bring you the results you are paid to achieve.

3. *You* Can't Motivate Anyone!

Many of you may be puzzled at this statement. You may be thinking, *I thought my primary job as a manager was motivating my team? I have motivation meetings, and everything I do is to motivate my team to achieve their goals!* From my perspective, you can't motivate anyone. Long-term employee motivation is the job of the employee! Motivation is an internal, personal thing. All a successful sales manager can do is to *create the environment* that allows people to motivate themselves. I classify motivation into three generic categories.

a. *Fear (the stick).* Fear may be effective in the short term, but eagles won't stick around under this style.
b. *Incentive (the carrot).* Incentives might provide some short-term results, but you can't continue to throw rewards and money at every problem. Incentives will eventually lose their effectiveness.
c. *Growth (the long-term secret).* Your best people want to continue to grow and develop. Eagles want to soar higher and be better. Focus on giving your best people room and opportunity to grow.

Motivation is truly an internal discipline. As Zig Ziglar has said, "Motivation is not permanent. But neither is bathing!" You constantly need to provide the tools and environment to keep your staff motivated. If all you do is to try to motivate everyone yourself, you will never succeed in the long term. Focus on creating an environment where your staff can grow, develop, and achieve, and you will achieve more of the results you are looking for. I am a believer in the power of the individual to control oneself, and the thought that my success is a result of the work that others do for me just does not sit right. Your best eagles will feel the same way. Give them room and opportunity to soar and do what they do best and you will get the results you want. "You can have everything in life you want if you will just help enough other people get what they want."

4. Poor Performance is the Sales Manager's Fault

Porter Henry, in his book, *Secrets of the Master Sales Managers*, says it this way: "Poor first-line management is the biggest cause of a slump. In 90% of the cases, the manager lets the rep get careless; isn't keeping the rep challenged; isn't working on the reps motivation." He also says, "No compensation plan is a substitute for effective sales management."

As a leader, you must take the responsibility for achieving your team's objectives. That is what you signed up for. That is your role and your responsibility. I like the following great comment from the ancient Greek philosopher Euripides: "Ten soldiers wisely led will beat a hundred without a head."

While I am a believer that the performance of the team is a direct reflection of the quality of the sales management, there are a number of negative outside factors that the sales manager cannot control. These are referred as the "Five D's." The sales manager is off the hook if the salesperson is suffering from poor performance due to any of these factors.

The Five D's of Poor Performance

- Drugs
- Drinking
- Divorce
- Disease
- Death

5. The Cmdr's Intent

In the military, they have developed a concept called the *commander's intent* (CI). This is the simple, overriding objective that the commander of an operation wants achieved. It helps to guide the specific tactics that all the various officers will develop to ensure that the mission is a success. All decisions are weighed against this simple commander's intent, and if the planned tactics are in line with the CI, then these plans will move the operation toward the ultimate goal.

It may come as no shock that I like this phrase, and thus I developed the Cmdr's Intent not only for our overall business but for the sales department. Here are my three points of the Cmdr's Intent for salespeople.

Cmdr's Intent for Sales

a. *Read.* Personal development and constant improvement are a common theme for me and throughout this book. It may surprise some in the sales field that this is my number-one intent. Reading (and other personal development) is the foundation of all growth and long-term development. Be a leader. Be a reader.

b. *Make the Calls.* This is not a revolutionary concept for sales staff. It drives at the heart of the managing activity focus. Sales is simply seeing people. Make the calls and you are well on the way.

c. *Use Testimonials: Especially Video.* I have long believed in the power of testimonials. Existing customers who have dealt with your company and suggest to others why they should do business with you are extremely credible and powerful. In today's age, video testimonials are an absolute requirement. Video is the killer app for the Internet, and it is estimated that by 2013, 90 percent of all consumer internet traffic will be video traffic. With the proliferation of YouTube, as well as cheap, high-quality video recorders, it is easy to have your customers tell other prospective clients about your company via video. It is powerful, and it works.

As the plaque with the bell that hangs on my wall says, "Nothing happens until somebody sells something." Effective sales management is the key to making the bell ring and keeping the company growing. I hope you glean a few ideas you can use in your own sales organization—or in any group of people, for that matter. Take the best, forget the rest. These ideas work. Just put them to use.

Parenting 101:
A Collection of Ideas for Parents

I am by no means a child psychology expert, nor do I think that I have been the perfect parent, but over the years, I have done a lot of thinking about how to be the best parent I can be. If some of the ideas below resonate with you and help you in your own relationship with your kids, I will have served you.

Up front, I must admit that I am more comfortable with girls than with boys. I was the oldest of five kids, with four younger sisters. I have two daughters, Tabitha and Nicole, and so all my child references and experiences have been around the females of our species. I have never been a macho type, or what people might consider a "man's man." I never played any organized sports growing up as a kid, except for a year or two of baseball when I was quite young. I am one of the few Canadian men who can't ice skate! I have had many strong female influences in my life, so if much of what you see below seems to apply more to females, I plead guilty as charged.

Scrapbooks

I credit Anthony Robbins for saying, "A life worth living is a life worth recording." I have believed this since I first started my own scrapbook on December 26, 1982, recording my first driving lesson in our green Ford Gran Torino station wagon. All my life's significant memories have been recorded in scrapbooks, and as of this writing, I am on volume 6.

Therefore, when our first daughter, Tabitha, was born, I started her scrapbook. It started with a photo of the house Tabitha was brought home to after she was born and the hospital bracelets that she and her mother wore. The newspaper headlines from the day she was born (November 19, 1993) pasted in her scrapbook read, "GST Will Go within Two Years, PM Vows." Tim Allen and the cast of *Home Improvement* were on the cover of the *TV Guide* that week, and the Toronto Maple Leafs were in first place overall in the NHL with 27 points! The Toronto 300 Composite index was at 4,291, the Dow Jones at 3,662, gold at $375.80 an ounce, and crude at $16.90 a barrel. Her first night out was a Saint John Flames vs. Portland Pirates AHL hockey game on December 4, 1993 (just a few weeks after she was born), and she has the ticket stub to prove it! You might not find any of these things that interesting, but they are significant parts of what life was like when she was born.

And this recording of life's events continues to this day. In their scrapbooks are things like the ticket stubs for every movie or concert they have ever attended. A lock of long hair after it was cut short. Art from school, certificates from school, letters from Santa, postcards, pictures—anything of any significance recorded in each girl's scrapbook. We have had many hours of fun looking back over the scrapbook, and today, about every four to six weeks, I pull out the most recent additions and add whatever new stuff we have collected.

So what is the big deal about a scrapbook? I believe keeping a scrapbook as your children are growing up is one of the most important things you can do for a number of reasons. If I know someone who is expecting a baby, I will buy that person a scrapbook for their child and "sell them" on why I think it is so important. So, let me explain why I am so passionate about scrapbooking.

Primarily it is about building your child's personal self-esteem. As they start to grow up, they are always interested in things about themselves. Keeping a book with all the things that they have done—one that is entirely about them—says that they are important. When family and friends came over, I would pull out the scrapbook and have the girls explain to the visitors what all the things in the book were. Invariably, the visitors would smile and talk to the girls about what was in the book. This taught girls to be comfortable talking with adults and showed them they were worth talking about.

Next, we all long for that connection with our past and our history. Over the years, as we periodically review the books, it amazes me how interested the girls are in all the little things they did, and some of the things or people that they have forgotten. It is easy to review all the positive things that have happened in the past and to feel good about ourselves doing so.

Beside each item in the scrapbook, I also write a note as if it were the girls writing it themselves. Here is just such an entry from Tabitha's first volume.

"January 15, 1998. My friend from school, Lachlan, just had a new baby sister born. She was 5 weeks early and was delivered in the bathroom! Lachlan told us the story and Mom visited Judy in the hospital. The story made front page news today."

Beside this was the newspaper clipping, with a photo of Judy Armstrong and Aidan that described the event. When the girls were too young to read and I would read the captions to them, and I could see them light up and engage even more.

On a selfish "Dad" level, I hope that when they are much older and look back on these books, they will see how much they were loved, and that Mom and Dad were not so bad after all! And I hope they realize that they had a pretty good time growing up! The practice of simply keeping a little shelf with scrapbook items (just above where I put the bills), updating their books every four to six weeks, is a simple act of service for my kids. I can't think of not doing it after all these years. This little act of service for the kids gives me great pleasure, and has had a positive impact on them as well.

Our Sand

In our living room, we had a large bowl filled with sand. In this sand, we would put small trinkets or items that we got while on family vacation. A red rock from our trip to Arizona. A lapel pin with a cannon from our trip to Gettysburg. A miniature Statue of Liberty from our trip to New York City. These are simple little things that are easy and inexpensive to pick up to remember a trip. We place them in the sand, and they become quite the conversation piece for our guests. Again, this gives the girls a chance to talk to adults about what they saw and learned on the trip. The sand bowl soon got crowded, and so we had a coffee table with a two-inch lip built that contains the sand that allows more items to be displayed. It is an easy way to create memories, and more importantly, it gives the kids another opportunity to develop communication and interaction skills with others.

Many of our family adventures are illustrated in the sand table in our family room.

Happy First Day of School!

Since the girls started school, on the first day of school I make them breakfast. I cut out the number of the grade they are going into out of a piece of toast and present their breakfast with a candle as I sing "Happy First Day of School" to the tune of Happy Birthday. Tabitha is now in grade 12 and Nicole in grade 9, and although they roll their eyes when I do it, I know the girls get a kick out of it. A simple, no-cost way to say "I love you" and your special day is important to me. I am already priming them to tell their university roommates to expect this for all the years they are in university!

Do You Love Me?

There are a number of great ideas that I took from a great book, *She Calls Me Daddy* by Robert Wolgemuth. One of our favourites is the hand squeeze sequence to show how much we love each other.

It starts with one person squeezing the other's hand four times, one time for each of the words "Do you love me?" The other person squeezes three times, meaning "Yes, I do." It goes back to the first person, who squeezes two times, meaning, "How much?" Then the other squeezes as hard as they can to show how much they love you!

I have been doing this with the girls for almost ten years; we can be walking, just holding hands and doing this back and forth, silently of course. Sometimes the last person just gives a short soft squeeze as a tease, and then we both start laughing!

This is a simple way to tell your kids you love them without making a big public spectacle. Something that is more important when they get older and become more self-conscious. The author of the book talks about doing the hand squeeze when walking his daughter down the aisle—it was the only way he could tell her how much he loved her without crying on this, her special day. It is the simple things in life that often mean the most to us.

Hello, Family!

The first thing I do when I come home is to call out, "Hello, family" and then come in and give each person a kiss and a hug to tell them how much I love them. I do this to make the point that they are the most important part of my life and I can't wait to see and embrace them. With teenage girls, they can get a little stingy with the kisses, but I know they know it means I love them. And I keep doing it every time, reinforcing this point every day.

I have carried this over to when we have our nieces and nephews come over to visit. As crazy Uncle Alex, I go over the top with enthusiasm when they are at the door of our house coming to visit. I run to the door, jumping up and down, and grab each kid and give them a big hug and lift them up! Our nieces, twin girls, scream with delight and try to hide behind their parents, but they love the attention. It does not take much to build the self-esteem of kids and show them that they are loved.

Millennium Notes

At the turn of the millennium in 1999, I came up with the idea of having all the girls' relatives (aunts, uncles, grandparents, etc.) write two little notes to each of the girls. The first would be opened on their sixteenth birthday (when they were officially young women), and the second would be opened on the day they got married. These would be notes of advice, thoughts, humour—whatever they wanted to say to them. I then had the notes sealed in separate envelopes and locked in a fireproof box.

The significance of such a simple act should not be understated. Since that time, 1999, when the girls were just seven and four, two of their grandfathers as well as their Auntie Bobbie have passed away. So on these two "milestone" days in the girls' lives, not only will they get these expressions of advice and love from these family members through their notes, but they will hear the voices of those departed loved ones giving them blessings and thoughts. It is my fondest hope that these notes become some of my girls' most prized possessions. Tears well up in my eyes every time I tell people about this idea. November 19, 2009, when Tabitha turned sixteen, was the first time we opened one of the letters. As expected, it was a positive and emotional event.

On a fun note in this vein, I also interviewed the girls and asked them questions that I recorded to be opened on their wedding day. Fun, light questions, like,

- Who will you marry?
- How many kids will you have?
- What do you think would be good names for your kids?
- What will you wear on your wedding day?
- Where do you want to live?

These should be very enjoyable and funny to read, as they were recorded by a four or seven year old, and will be opened some twenty years later! I can only imagine the fun we will have with that.

This simple idea of having family and loved ones write a note to be opened later guarantees that the love and message they want to give are able to be conveyed. It costs nothing, just some time and effort, and yet I think this simple act of service could be one of the most significant things you could do for your children.

I Try...

As I write this, I know I am not the best Dad in the world. I am not an expert in parenting, and people don't seek me out for my sage wisdom about being a parent. However, I have tried to take actions and do things that build up my kids and show them the unconditional love I have for them. And I want them to live their own lives as best they can with the foundational basis of unconditional love that a parent can give.

I often say that all a parent can do is provide their children with values and experiences. If, by the time my child is eighteen and becomes an adult, if they have not learned values (respect, work ethic, spiritual values, etc.) and had a variety of experiences to broaden their perspective on life, then I will have failed as a parent. I want my girls to become their own individual people and make their future life decisions based on what they truly want. One of the quotes on the idea canvas is from psychologist Carl Jung: "The greatest burden a child must bear is the unlived lives of their parents." I promise my kids to live a great, full life and relieve them of this burden!

The Lessons of the Pump

I n my office, for over fifteen years, I have had a cast iron water pump with a little brass plaque on the base, which reads, "Understanding the Lessons of the Pump will Reveal the Secrets of Success." This story is in tribute to two of the strongest influences in my personal and professional life. The first is Zig Ziglar, from whom I liberally stole this story, and the second is my first mentor, Cecil Van Buskirk. While I spent only three years working with Cecil during my time at Atlantic Speedy Propane, I feel I learned more in those three years than many people have in a career.

The Story of the Pump

It was a hot August afternoon, and Cecil and I were riding back from a management meeting in Moncton toward Saint John, both in New

The Pump

Brunswick, Canada. I was the General Sales Manager for Atlantic Speedy Propane, a wholly owned division of Irving Oil that sold all propane equipment and fuel throughout Atlantic Canada. Cecil had recruited me earlier that year from my job as a product manager for CFM (Canadian Fireplace Manufacturers.) As part of my role at CFM, I had taken on the Speedy account, and I had grown the fireplace sales business for CFM with Speedy from thirty units to over three hundred units in less than a year. Cecil had hired me to become the General Sales Manager, working from the home office in Moncton and responsible for the sales activities of thirty-five branch managers and salespeople in twenty-eight branches in the four Atlantic Provinces of Canada.

I had never been a real sales person before, yet alone a sales manager, and here I was at twenty-seven years old with a big responsibility. Cecil was not my boss. In fact, he did not even work for Speedy Propane. He worked for another Irving company, Maritime Tire. However, Cecil had worked for Irving for over thirty-five years in many jobs, and his latest responsibility involved overseeing the activities of Speedy Propane, working closely with our general manager, Doug Goddard. Cecil did not have title power, per se, but it was clear that he was someone you listened and responded to. I was very lucky to have Cecil overseeing me, as I learned a lot from him. And on this hot August day, I did not know it, but I was in for quite a lesson.

We were driving back that hot afternoon, and I was parched. I said to Cecil that we needed to stop to get a drink or I did not think I would make it back to Saint John. Cecil, who had travelled these roads for over thirty-five years, told me to pull off the highway. We would find an old abandoned farmhouse near a pond that had an old water pump outside and we could get a drink there.

I pulled up to the old house, clearly in a poor state of repair, and saw the black cast iron pump by the side of the house. I turned off the car, jumped out, and ran to the pump. I started pumping and pumping, fast and furious, but nothing was happening. I continued to pump, but still nothing happening. As I glanced up, I saw Cecil walking toward me shaking his head with disappointment as only he could. As he walked closer he said, "Alex, clearly you are a city boy. Don't you know anything about working these old pumps?"

"Well," I replied, "don't you just take this handle and pump it up and down and the water comes out the spout?"

"Of course that is how it works. But everyone knows you have to prime the pump first!"

"Prime the pump? How do I do that?" I asked.

"In order for the pump to work," Cecil responded, "you have to put a little water in the spout to wet the seal and make it airtight so the pumping action will work."

He walked down to the pond and took out some of the water in an old rusty bucket. He then poured a bit of water into the spout of the pump. I did not know it at the time, but this was the first lesson of the pump.

With the pump primed, I continued to pump. I pumped and pumped and pumped, but still no water was coming out. I looked over and saw Cecil smiling at me. "Cecil, I don't think there is any water here. I think this well has gone dry."

With a knowing look, Cecil replied, "In this part of the province, the wells are really deep, and the locals are happy about that. Do you know why they are happy about having to dig such deep wells?" I did not know so he continued. "Around here the wells are deep, and the deeper the well, the longer it takes for the groundwater to get to it. By the time it has gone down so far, the earth has filtered out any impurities and all that remains is the best, purest, coldest water you can find. If the wells were shallow, all the impurities from the air pollution and the roads would get into their water. The deeper the well, the better tasting the water."

This advice would turn out to be the second lesson of the pump.

Finally, after about ten minutes of pumping, sweating in the hot August sun with no results, I stopped pumping, threw up my hands and exclaimed in frustration, "There is no water here! This well has gone dry!" Cecil immediately jumped past me and grabbed the pump handle. He continued to pump, so that no real time had elapsed from when I stopped and he had started. "Now listen to me, Alex. You can't give up pumping once you get started. Who knows how far up the well the water has risen? And if you stop, it will fall all the way to the bottom and you will have to start all over again. We don't want to do the work twice now, do we?" As I thought about this, I saw the wisdom in Cecil's words. That turned out to be the third lesson of the pump.

Cecil continued, "Once you start pumping, you just keep going! You never stop! You just keep pumping and pumping and pumping and keep working at it!" By now Cecil was pumping faster, with greater effort than I had given, and I was no slouch in my work ethic! I was thirsty and wanted water! But as he kept up the activity, the water soon started to flow. Cecil slowed down his pace, never stopping, but not pumping as hard or fast as he had been. "You see," he said, "if you just keep pumping and pumping, the water will start to flow.

And once it starts flowing, all you need is a little easy, steady pressure and you will have more water than you could ever imagine." And as I dipped my hands into the cold, pure water coming from the pump, I realized that this was the fourth and final lesson of the pump.

The four lessons of the pump really do reveal the secrets of success.

Lesson #1 – You Have to Put Something In before You Can Get Something Out

In order to get the water from the pump, you have to prime it—that is put a little water in so that you can get a lot of water out. This is the way of life. You must put in some effort or time or capital into any project or activity before you can expect to get something out of it. You don't stand at the woodstove of life and demand, "Hey, you give me some heat and I will put in the wood." You have to put the wood in first! If you want to get ahead in your career, you have to put in the time and effort first, before you expect any results. Put in first before you expect anything out.

Lesson #2 – The Longer You Work At Something, the More Rewarding It Is

The pump story illustrates that a deep well has water that is clean, filtered and pure by the time it comes out at the spout. If things came easy, then everyone could do them, and there would be no reward or satisfaction in doing them. When you have to work hard and long at a problem or project, when you are finally finished, you have that great satisfaction of accomplishing something. You feel the pride in your success. Too often we want the quick fix. These fast and easy results are never the ones that last. It took Michelangelo many years to paint the Sistine Chapel, and hundreds of years later, we appreciate his work. Malcolm Gladwell, in his book *The Outliers*, talks about the ten-thousand-hour rule: to become a master of any activity, it takes more than ten thousand hours of effort. Keep pumping—it is worth it.

Lesson #3 – Never, Never Quit!

The pump simply shows why you should never quit. If you pump and the water is just at the top of the well and you quit, the water flows all the way back down. If you want to get the water, you have to start all over again and repeat the same process to get it to just where you stopped. If you had only gone a little further, pumped a little more, you would have all the water you want. There is a great saying I learned many years ago: "Anything worth doing is worth doing poorly, until you can learn to do it well!" When you first start anything, you won't be very good at it, be it piano, golf, sales, or any other activity. You have to keep trying and keep going, learning every step of the way. By the effort and the mistakes you make, you learn the skill and it ends up becoming effortless.

There are four stages of competence everyone has to go through when they take on any new project or task.

1. *Unconscious incompetence.* You don't know that you don't know! You are unaware of what it is you should be doing.

2. *Conscious incompetence.* You know that you don't know what you are doing, and you get frustrated as you start learning. You trip and fall, and get poor results, but you keep at it.

3. *Conscious competence.* You know that you know what you are doing, but you have to think about it. Hold my head down, bend my knees, breathe deep, swing easy. You are getting results, but you have to think about what you are doing.

4. *Unconscious competence.* You don't even have to think about being good. Do you think Tiger Woods thinks about where to put his feet or his hands when he swings a golf club?

As you invest the time in getting good at whatever you do, keep this in mind and never, never quit. Soon, you will be so good you don't even have to think about it!

Lesson #4 – It Gets Easier, but You Never Stop!

As the story of the pump so elegantly shows, once the water is starting to flow, you just keep that simple up-and-down pumping motion going, and the water will flow forever. Notice that you don't have to work as hard as you did at the beginning, but also notice you are still pumping! Consider an airplane. An airplane has to go down the runway for takeoff at full throttle in order to get up into the air. However, once it gets to its cruising altitude, the pilot then eases back on the throttle and can fly for thousands of miles. If he did not back off the throttle, he would burn out the engines and use up all his fuel.

Once you get good at what you are doing, it is easier, as you have spent the time preparing and working hard. But you can't stop; you must keep going. If you think you will be able to stop studying and learning once you finish school, you are mistaken! Education is ongoing. Would you want a doctor to operate on you who had not read a medical book or received any training since graduating twenty years ago? If not, then why would you stop learning in your field? This does not mean you need to study full time, like when you were at school, but ongoing education is a lifetime commitment if you want to keep the water flowing. Stop learning, stop pumping, and the well soon dries up.

I love to tell this story and bring out my pump. It is a simple yet profound story, and I want to thank Zig for the inspiration. It was at his suggestion that I get a pump, and so I did. And I have been pumping ever since!

Cmdr Pettes and his pump!

Final Comments

Thank you for taking your time to read these words. I hope this book has been of some benefit, giving you a few ideas that you can use in your life or business.

As I said in the beginning, the journey of personal self-discovery I have gone through has been of tremendous significance to me. I have learned much, refining my thinking, and hope that this has been of service to you in a small way. It is my personal mission that "I AM having everything I want in life as I help and serve enough other people get what they want." I am on that path, and am glad this book is finally complete! I wish you great success and service to others in your life.

Keep Super Good!

Cmdr Pettes